AIR SPORTS

Ellen Labrecque

Raintree

Chicago, Illinois

www.heinemannraintree.com
Visit our website to find out more information about Heinemann-Raintree books.

To order:
☎ Phone 888-454-2279
💻 Visit www.heinemannraintree.com to browse our catalog and order online.

Edited by Rebecca Rissman, Dan Nunn, and Catherine Veitch
Designed by Joanna Hinton Malivoire
Picture research by Ruth Blair
Originated by Capstone Global Library
Printed and bound in China by CTPS

15 14 13 12 11
10 9 8 7 6 5 4 3 2 1

Library of Congress Cataloging-in-Publication Data
Labrecque, Ellen.
  Air sports / Ellen Labrecque.
    p. cm.—(Extreme sports)
  Includes bibliographical references and index.
  ISBN 978-1-4109-4215-9 (hardcover)—ISBN 978-1-4109-4222-7 (pbk.) 1. Aeronautical sports—Juvenile literature. I. Title.
  GV755.L33 2012
  797.5—dc22   2010042309

Acknowledgments
We would like to thank the following for permission to reproduce photographs: Alamy pp. 15 (© Alun Richardson), 22 (© David Sims); Corbis pp. 5 (© Ken Glaser), 6 (© Benelux), 7 (© Bettmann), 9 (© Alain Revel, Rene Robert, Jean-Luc Boivin/Sygma), 10 (© HO/Reuters), 12 (© Jim Sugar), 13 (© Kevin Fleming), 21 (© Mark Newman—Rainbow/Science Faction), 24 (© Photo Japan/Robert Harding World Imagery), 25 (© Alessandro Bianchi/Reuters), 26 (© Sam Diephuis); Getty Images pp. 8 (Bob Bird), 11 (Helmut Tucek), 19 (Dean Mouhtaropoulos); Shutterstock pp. 4 (© Germanskydiver), 14 (© Aleksandar Todorovic), 16 (© Graham Prentice), 17 (© Mihai Dancaescu), 18 (© homydesign), 20 (© JanJar), 23 (© Oleksii Abramov), 27 (© Germanskydiver), 28 (© G Tipene), 29 (© Monkey Business Images).

Cover photograph of skydivers jumping from an airplane reproduced with permission of Corbis (© Moodboard).

Every effort has been made to contact copyright holders of material reproduced in this book. Any omissions will be rectified in subsequent printings if notice is given to the publisher.

All the Internet addresses (URLs) given in this book were valid at the time of going to press. However, due to the dynamic nature of the Internet, some addresses may have changed, or sites may have changed or ceased to exist since publication. While the author and publisher regret any inconvenience this may cause readers, no responsibility for any such changes can be accepted by either the author or the publisher.

Some words are shown in bold, **like this**. You can find out what they mean by looking in the glossary.

Contents

What Are Air Sports?

Welcome to the thrilling world of air sports. This is a world where competitors **soar** above the earth and people actually fly!

STAY SAFE!
Remember that many of these sports should be left to the **experts**!

Skydiving

Want to touch the clouds? Then give skydiving a try. Skydiving is when a person jumps from a moving aircraft. After **free falling** through the air, the jumper opens a parachute and comes to a soft landing.

WOW!

Joseph Kittinger holds the record for the highest, fastest, and longest skydive. In 1960 he jumped from an aircraft and reached speeds of 614 miles per hour!

BASE Jumping

BASE jumping is like skydiving, but more dangerous. A jumper leaps from a fixed object, such as a building, a bridge, or a cliff. The jumper has just seconds to open a parachute.

Wingsuit Flying

Want to fly through the air like a superhero? In wingsuit flying, athletes put on a special wingsuit made from **fabric**. The suit helps lift up the body. A flight ends with a parachute opening so the flyer can land safely.

WOW!

In 2003 Austrian daredevil Felix Baumgartner flew across the English Channel in a wingsuit. He traveled at 224 miles per hour. That's the same speed as a racing car!

Hang Gliding

A hang gliding pilot flies an aircraft without a motor. The pilot is **suspended** in a **harness** below the hang glider. The pilot takes off by pushing off the ground with his or her feet. The pilot steers by moving his or her body.

WOW!

Hang gliders can **soar** hundreds of miles for hours at a time. The longest flight on record is more than 11 hours!

Paragliding

Paragliding and hang gliding are similar. Both have a pilot who sits in a **harness** underneath a **fabric** wing. But a paraglider is like a parachute, while a hang glider has a metal frame.

WOW!

The farthest a paraglider has ever flown is 313 miles. That is about the length of the state of Georgia!

Gliding

Imagine flying your own plane ... without an engine! To get **soaring**, the glider is pulled with a **towrope** by a powered aircraft. Once released, the glider can soar for hundreds of miles.

glider

WOW!
Gliding competitions are held all over the world. There are racing and **aerobatic** competitions. In aerobatic competitions, gliders perform tricks.

Air Racing

Get your eyes on the sky! Air racing involves small aircraft racing one another through air gates. The aircraft only fly about **66** feet in the air, so fans can watch closely. The pilots are fast and skilled. If they miss the gates, they are **penalized**.

air gate

WOW!
In New York City in June 2010, pilots raced around the Statue of Liberty!

Hot Air Ballooning

People have been flying in hot air balloons for more than 200 years. Hot air balloons are powered by hot air shot through a burner. The hot air helps the balloon rise through the cooler air.

WOW!

In 1999 two men flew a hot air balloon around the world. It took them just under 20 days to complete the trip.

Kite Surfing

Kite surfing is also called kite boarding. A kite surfer hooks his or her feet onto a small surfboard. The surfer is pulled through the water by a kite and the wind!

WOW!

Kirsty Jones of Wales holds the kite surfing distance world record. She traveled from an island near Spain to Morocco in Africa. The trip took more than nine hours!

Kite Fighting

Kite fighting is serious business in many Asian countries. The object of a fight is to cut the other person's string and knock the kite down. Kite fighting can be one-on-one, or among a lot of people. The kite left flying is the winner.

WOW!

Fighter kites are made with strings of munja. Munja is a type of grass that is as sharp as a razor blade.

Be Safe!

Air sports can be exciting, wild, and thrilling. But they can also be dangerous and scary.

Do not try any of these sports on your own. Listen to **experts** and take many lessons before trying these sports. You must always make sure you wear all the proper **equipment** needed for a safe ride.

Get Fit!

Having strong arms is important for many sports. The stronger arms and shoulders you have, the better athlete you will be. Try this arm exercise.

From a standing position, extend your arms straight out from your body. **Rotate** your arms in a forward motion making small circles. Gradually increase the size of the circles until you are making big circles. Do this for two to four minutes at a time.

Glossary

aerobatics stunts performed in flight

equipment tools or clothing that you need

expert person with a special skill or knowledge

fabric cloth made by weaving or knitting

free falling fall from something very quickly, from a great height

harness safety equipment and straps used to support someone

penalized punished or put at a disadvantage. For example, an athlete may be penalized for doing something wrong, and so extra time is added to his or her race time.

rotate turn around a central point

soar fly or rise up high into the air

suspended hang by attachment to something

towrope strong line used to pull something along

Find Out More

Books

Gale, Lesley. *Ultimate Thrill Sports: Skydiving*.
 Pleasantville, N.Y.: Gareth Stevens, 2008.

Hamilton, Sue L. *Xtreme Sports: Base Jumping*.
 Edina, Minn.: Abdo, 2010.

Hicks, Kelli Shay. *Action Sports: Hot Air Ballooning*.
 Vero Beach, Fla.: Rourke, 2010.

Whittall, Noel. *Ultimate Thrill Sports: Hang Gliding*.
 Pleasantville, N.Y.: Gareth Stevens, 2008.

Websites

www.kidnetic.com
This website has lots of information about healthy
eating and exercise. Why not get fit and enjoy
some extreme sports?

**http://kidshealth.org/kid/stay_healthy/food/
sports.html**
Find out more about eating well and playing
sports.

www.nationalkitemonth.org/kids/howtofly.shtml
Learn some tips and tricks for flying a kite.

Index